Buried Treasure

Written by Juliet Kerrigan
Illustrated by Fred Blunt

Contents

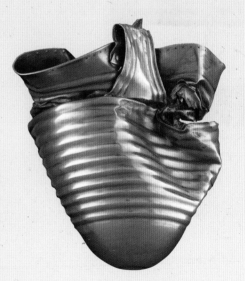

Collins

What is treasure and how do you find it?

We're going on a treasure hunt, but how can we tell what is valuable? Gold, silver and gems are valuable, but what about animal bones and cloth? They may not look like treasure, but they can tell us how people lived long ago.

When something has been buried in the ground for
a long time, it may change colour and shape.

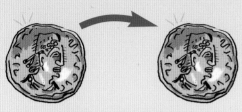

Gold stays shiny.

*Silver turns purple-grey
and may break.*

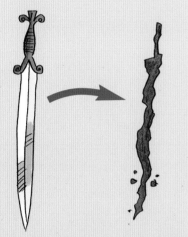

Iron turns into rusty lumps.

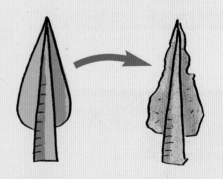

Copper and bronze go green.

Bones may crumble.

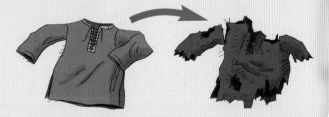

*Cloth survives only in very hot,
very cold and very wet places.*

Anyone can find buried treasure, but you need
an archaeologist to tell you more about it.
Archaeologists study the past using objects that have been
dug up. Buried treasure may tell us *what* happened
in the past, *when* it happened and sometimes *why*.

An archaeologist's tool kit

On the dig

 *trowel*

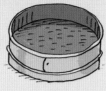 *sieve*

 *brush*

 pegs

 string

Recording the treasure

 *bag*

 *label*

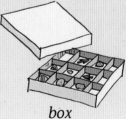 *box*

 *camera*

 notebook

Flint hand axe

This piece of **flint** was found buried on a beach in England. It's a hand axe and it's 500,000 years old. You can tell it's a hand axe by looking at the shape of the stone and the sharp point at the top. It was made at a time when people made tools out of stone, not metal.

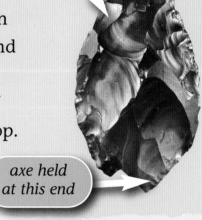

sharp edge for cutting

axe held at this end

Flint tools were sharp enough to cut down trees.

Bone flute

Archaeologists found a flute made from a **vulture** bone, buried in a cave in Germany. It is 33,000 years old and shows that thousands of years ago, people may have listened to music, just like we do today.

The hand axe and the flute were both made in a time called the Stone Age.

Gold cup

Later, people started making things with metal. Although this cup has been bent by a farmer's plough, archaeologists can tell it has been made from a single piece of gold. It's over 4,000 years old, and may have been used on a special occasion.

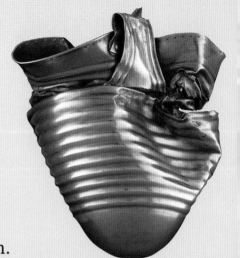

The gold cup may have been used to drink from.

Metal axe-heads

These metal axe-heads were found in a field in England. They are 3,000 years old. They never had wooden handles, so they may have been used instead of money for buying things.

The gold cup and the metal axe-heads were both made in a time called the Bronze Age.

One sheep, please!

Gold coins

As time went on, people began using coins. When archaeologists found the leg bone of a cow it looked very ordinary. But when an **X-ray** was taken, 20 gold coins were shown buried inside it. This treasure was hidden, and then forgotten … for 2,000 years!

Coins like these have also been found in France. Perhaps their owner travelled to France, and brought the coins back to Britain.

Britain

France

Horses may have been important to the people who made the coins.

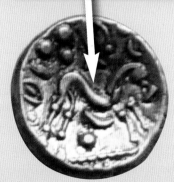

The gold coins were used in a time called the Iron Age.

Silver pepper pot

As people started to travel more, spices like cinnamon, ginger and pepper were brought from India and Sri Lanka. The spices were sold at the local markets.

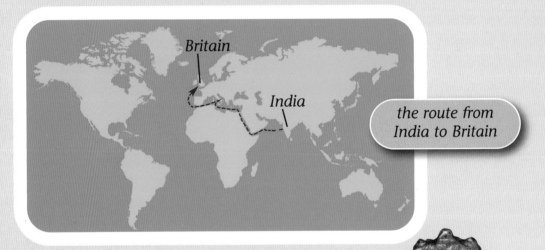

the route from India to Britain

This silver pepper pot was found buried in a field in Britain. It shows that 1,600 years ago, people used pepper at mealtimes. It has been made in the shape of a Roman lady and it shows the hairstyle, jewellery and clothes that were worn by rich people.

The silver pepper pot was made in Roman times.

A Roman feast

olives, tuna fish, sliced egg

~

broccoli, lamb, fish

~

grapes, pears,
roasted chestnuts

Rich Romans didn't sit at the table
to eat. They lay on couches.

13

Bronze helmet

Only an important person would have owned an iron and bronze helmet like this, decorated with a dragon's head. It was found in a grave, and had to be pieced together like a jigsaw. The helmet is 1,400 years old.

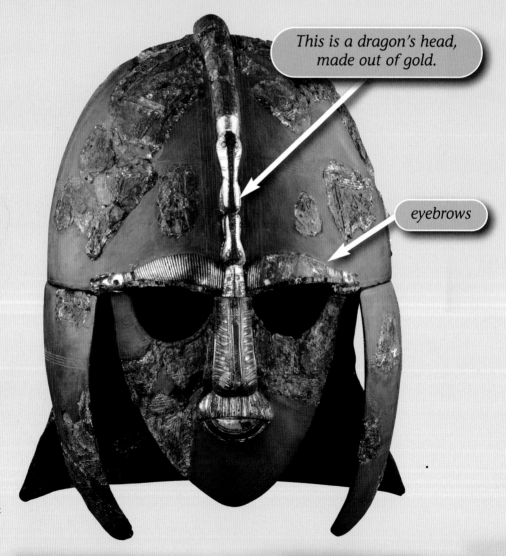

This is a dragon's head, made out of gold.

eyebrows

Bead necklace

Ordinary people were buried with objects, like this necklace. Each bead may have been added at a different time, like a modern charm bracelet. One of the beads is much older than the others, which shows that people made jewellery using old and new materials.

This is the oldest bead in the necklace.

The bronze helmet and the bead necklace were both made in Anglo-Saxon times.

Curious clothing

These shoes, hat and cape were found frozen with the 5,000-year-old body of a man. The type of clothing shows that the man may have been a shepherd. These clothes were designed for icy weather, and the straps on the soles of the shoes would have helped the man to climb mountains.

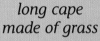
leather cap lined with fur

long cape made of grass

leather shoes lined with grass, with leather straps on the soles

A 3,000-year-old miniskirt was found in the grave of a woman in Denmark. It's made of one long strand of wool, and must have taken many hours to make. This shows the skirt was owned by someone rich or important. It may have been worn over another piece of clothing.

The skirt has a belt with a tassel.

What are you wearing?

Weird food

Butter that is thousands of years old has been found buried in Irish and Scottish **peat bogs**. It may have been buried to keep it cool, or hidden because it was valuable to its owner. It's valuable to archaeologists because they can study real food from the past. The oldest butter found was buried nearly 3,000 years ago, and 500 tubs have been found so far!

The butter is now grey, not yellow. Would you eat it?

The butter has been found buried in wooden tubs, wicker baskets, animal skins, cloth and bark.

Glossary

a dig   a place where archaeologists are investigating

flint   hard stone that can be sharpened to make tools and weapons

peat bogs   very wet, muddy places made from old rotting plants and trees

vulture   a large bird of prey

X-ray   a special photograph that shows something you can't see – for example, bones in a body

Index

Treasure timeline

33,000 years ago

3,000 years ago

2,000 years ago

1,600 years ago

1,400 years ago

now

Ideas for reading

Written by Clare Dowdall
Lecturer and Primary Literacy Consultant

Learning objectives: draw together ideas and information from across a whole text, using simple signposts in the text; explain organisational features of texts, including alphabetical order, layout, diagrams, captions; explain their reactions to texts, commenting on important aspects; listen to others in class, ask relevant questions and follow instructions

Curriculum links: History: What was it like to live here in the past? Citizenship: Living in a diverse world

Interest words: treasure, archaeologist, valuable, flint, vulture, plough, occasion, cinnamon, tassel, peat

Word count: 956

Resources: ICT

Getting started

- Read the blurb together, noting that this is an information book. Ask children to suggest the features that may be included in an information text, e.g. photographs and captions, lists, headings, contents, index.

- Look at the word *archaeologist*. Remind children of the different strategies that they can use to read new and unfamiliar words, e.g. sounding out, looking for parts of a word that they recognise, using contextual knowledge.

- Turn to the contents. Read the contents through with the children.

Reading and responding

- Read pp2–3 aloud with the children. Ask children to describe what has happened to each item of treasure in the pictures on p3.

- Return to the contents and ask children to use the contents to select a subject that interests them to read about independently.

- Listen to and support children as they read aloud quietly. Praise them for using a range of strategies for decoding. Help children with new and unfamiliar words.

- Ask children to continue reading, using the contents to select topics of interest.